Go GENErals FOR kids

VOLUME 5
EVAN ROBERTS

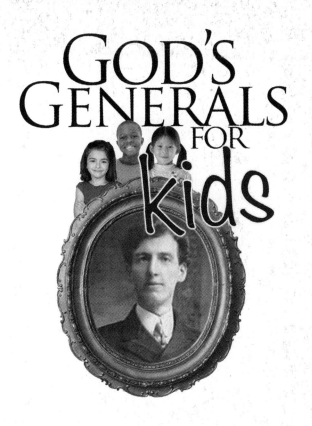

GOD'S GENERALS FOR Kids

VOLUME 5
EVAN ROBERTS

Lewis

ROBERTS LIARDON &
OLLY GOLDENBERG

Bridge-Logos
Alachua, Florida 32615 USA

Bridge-Logos

Alachua, Florida 32615 USA

God's Generals For Kids — Evan Roberts

Roberts Liardon & Olly Goldenberg

Printed in the United States of America.

Library of Congress Catalog Card Number: 2014934642
International Standard Book Number 978-1-61036-128-6

Unless otherwise noted, all Scripture is from the King James Version of the Bible.

The photographs used are owned by and taken from the private collection of Roberts Liardon.

Timeline illustrations by David Parfitt.

VP 3-20-14

Contents

Timeline

1890

May 7th 1878 Born

1878

October 31st 1904

1890 Starts work in mines

1902 Apprentice to blacksmith

1902

Sept. 13th 1904 Begins minister's training

Oct. 31st 1904 Revival begins

1905 4th nervous breakdown. Goes to live in England with Mrs. Penn Lewis

1914

September 13th 1904

1905

1914 1st World War starts

1925 Starts writing in Brighton

1927

1927 Moves back to Cardiff

1925

1928 A small revival

1951 Goes to heaven

1878–1951 1951

1928

Chapter 1
A Unique Child
★ ★ ★ ★

Young Evan

Something Different

Have you ever felt like you didn't fit in with others? Perhaps you were at a party or at school and you felt different from everyone else in the room. Evan Roberts always felt there was something different about himself, even as a young boy.

Evan was born in Wales, on May 7, 1878. His parents loved Jesus and went to a Methodist Church called Moriah Chapel. He was christened when he was young and they taught him about God. But they had no idea that God was going to use him to minister across Wales and around the world.

When he was a little boy, Evan loved to play. He stood out from the other children because his hair was curly and fair. He also stood out because of the way he played with others.

Sometimes they would be playing a game of chase. Then, right in the middle of the game, Evan would stop. He wasn't too tired to run; he just wanted to enjoy the world around him. "These birds are beautiful," he would say to no one in particular. And he would stand there listening while the birds sang. Evan loved nature.

He also loved people.

Caring for Others

Evan only wanted to play if everyone around him was happy. If someone was left out or sad he would do his best to make them feel happy. He was always thinking about others and he only felt happy when everyone around him was happy.

One day he was playing with a group of children, when one of them fell over and was hurt. The other children made sure he was alright and then carried on with their game. Evan also checked to see if he was alright and then sat next to the boy until he was ready to join in again.

When Evan was four years old he went to school. His teachers soon found out that he was very clever. One year the teachers made an announcement: "We are going to have a test and the child who does the best in each grade will win a book."

Everyone knew that the book would be won by one of two boys, and one of those boys was Evan. When the day of the test came, Evan sat down picked up his pencil, began the test and did his best. The teacher marked the test and announced that Evan had won.

You can imagine how happy he was, when he won top of the class, and how excited he must have been walking home carrying the new book he had won. After all any ordinary child would feel that way.

But Evan didn't. When he got home he burst into tears.

"Oh Mommy," he sobbed, "It's not fair. That other boy nearly won this book, but didn't get anything. He must be feeling really sad."

Evan was always thinking about other people, that's just the way he was. Evan was always playing with, but never hurting other children. In fact, he always seemed to do the right thing.

One day during one of the lessons, the children were not listening to the teacher. "Sit down and be quiet please," she called. But nobody took any notice.

"Will you all sit down and be quiet," the teacher shouted again. But still nobody listened.

Evan walked to the front of the classroom, stood in front of all the children and said, "The teacher is asking us to be quiet so we should be." Some of the children laughed at him, but he kept on speaking. "If we keep being naughty we will not learn, and if we don't learn we will not go far in life. Everybody should sit down."

And they did.

Evan was always ready to stick up for the teachers and for what was right. He didn't care what other people thought about him, he only wanted to do the right thing.

Helping at Home

Evan also did the right thing at home. Whenever his parents asked him to help, Evan would jump up right away and help. Even though he loved playing, he would not stop working until the job was done.

Many children listen to their parents like this, but Evan went one step further. He found ways to help his parents even when they didn't ask him.

When Evan was 12 years old his mom gave birth to a little sister. It should have been a happy time, but Evan's mother became really sick after she had given birth. Nobody was sure if she would live or die. Evan's dad was busy worrying about his mom, so Evan often looked after his sister.

Sometimes his parents would ask him to go to a family friend and pass on a message. Knowing what his parents wanted him to do Evan would run as fast as he could, to obey his parents.

One day, as Evan was looking after and holding his baby sister, he looked out the window into their garden. It was not a pretty sight. The garden was in a real mess. His dad had been so worried about the family that he hadn't had time to look after the garden.

Evan decided to do something about it. For the next few days he dug and pulled out the weeds and cleaned up the garden, and didn't stop until he had finished the job he had given himself to do for his Dad.

Evan really was unique. Throughout his childhood he was always clean, tidy and polite. He was also very clever. In fact it was his clever, quick-thinking that would soon make him a hero to his younger brother Dan.

Saving Others

One day Evan was playing and washing in a stream with his friends and brother. A group of the boys had gathered around one boy, Jenkin Evans. "I dare you to swim across the stream," one of the boys said to Jenkin.

"You can do it, for sure," another boy pitched in.

The stream was cold and deep and the water was flowing very fast, but Jenkin didn't want to let them down. He jumped into the water and started to swim across. The boys all stood on the side cheering him on, but Jenkin didn't even get half way across when he started to sink.

His head was right under the water, and he came to the surface again, but only for a few seconds.

Evan saw at once that Jenkin was in trouble. He threw off his outer clothes and waded into the stream. Jenkin's head popped up one more time. His voice was full of panic, "Help! Help I'm drowning!" And with that he sank back underwater. By now Evan had nearly reached him.

Evan had never learned to swim, in fact this was his first time to try swimming, but as usual Evan wasn't thinking about himself. When he reached Jenkin, he grabbed him around the neck.

Now both boys went underwater together. Evan knew that he could help; he didn't know that both of them could have drowned. As his feet touched the bottom he pushed himself up, dragging Jenkin with him. He hauled Jenkin to the bank, helped him up and then climbed up himself.

Back on the shore Jenkin was still panicking. The other boys gathered around, some were hysterical. But Evan was still completely calm. He had rescued Jenkin before any of the other boys had even realized what was going on.

When his brother Dan was bathing in the

stream a few months later, Evan kept a close eye on him. Suddenly something started to drag Dan under the water. Evan didn't even hesitate but leapt in after his brother and saved his life too. Evan became Dan's hero.

Playing Church

The other children all knew that there was something different about Evan. He had courage, he cared for people, he was clever and he was good. People liked Evan, but sometimes he didn't want to play with them. Instead he would stay home all day to read a book and look after his baby sister.

He was so different from the other children. They could have teased him because he was different, but they didn't because everyone knew he was the hero who had saved other people's lives. That's why they would join him when he invited them to play his favorite game: "church."

Evan would sit with his friends to have a

service with them. As the children met together they would sing hymns, Evan would share Bible verses and explain them to the other children. He was a leader among his friends and he loved leading them to Jesus.

In the evenings Evan would sit with his mom as she taught him memory verses and prayed with him. He learned as much as he could from her so that he would have more things to tell his friends about Jesus.

God was already using Evan and he hadn't even started his life work yet.

Chapter 2
The Young Man Matures

★ ★ ★ ★

Evans Parents

Starting Work

Evan's dad worked in the coal mine. He had a really important job working a pump. So when he broke his leg in an accident it was really serious. He couldn't do his job until it got better. No job would mean no money, and no money would mean no food for the family.

Evan was only 11 and a half years old, but he had to leave school to help.

Each day he would go to work at the coal mine with his dad and work the pump. After a few months his dad's leg was better and Evan was given a proper job in the mine. Now he had to work to earn money. At the age of twelve his childhood was over.

Each morning he would put on his helmet and take his lamp with him as he was lowered underground into the darkness of the mine.

As with all new workers, Evan started work as a door boy. Whenever a truck full of coal passed by on the rails, Evan had to open the door for it. When the truck had gone past, Evan would close the door again. It wasn't a very exciting job, all day he would sit in the dark by himself waiting for a truck to go past. As it approached, he would leap up and open the door in time to stop it from crashing. If he didn't do it in time, he would have been in big trouble.

The miners would pass him on the way to work and on the way home again. Some would go past him more often as they took the coal to the surface. And Evan was always ready for them.

Whenever he was in the mine, Evan had his Bible with him. As people passed him he would read out a Bible verse for them to think about during the day. His childhood game of "church" was now becoming more serious.

When the miners returned he would stop them, "What did you learn from the Bible verse I read you?" The miners soon got used to the preacher boy and his strange habit.

Close to Death

One day Evan had just let a train of trucks through the door when he heard a rumbling sound. A truck had come loose from the others and was now hurtling back down towards him. If he didn't open the door in time it would crash. If he didn't move he would be crushed.

Using his same quick thinking that had helped him to save the lives of others, he pushed the door open. As Evan's dad looked on from a distance he could not see how Evan would survive. "Evan!" he called after him, but there was nothing he could do.

As the dust settled Evan could be seen grinning. There was not even a scratch on him and he had done his job well. Word of this near miss went around the mine.

"He must have been saved by God," some said.

"God really is with that preacher boy."

The pits were dangerous places to work. Nobody wanted to be a door boy for long. When the bosses realized how hard Evan worked they allowed him to start work in the mine itself, digging out the coal.

Taking God to Work

In the main part of the mine, Evan took his Bible with him. Of course he couldn't read it while he was digging, but he kept it in a crack in the rock, then whenever he had a break he could turn to it.

The other miners didn't know how to cope with Evan. He was polite, but he didn't let them swear or tell rude jokes. Even when they were talking about sports Evan wasn't interested. He would just sit there staring off into space thinking about God.

The miners didn't understand him, but they all agreed that God was with him. Evan knew that God had a special plan for his life too.

At the age of thirteen he started to write down his own story. After all if he was going to do great things people would want to know about his life. When his family heard he was writing a book they started to tease him, "You are so proud. Writing a book about yourself!"

Evan didn't want to be proud; he wanted to serve God, so he destroyed this book.

But when another book was almost destroyed he held on to it as the most important thing in his life. Evan turned up to work one morning to discover that there had been a huge explosion and fire in the mine. Evan's Bible was scorched but not burnt and could still be used. The pages had been scattered and Evan carefully picked up each one. For years to come he treasured that Bible.

But now the Bible was to challenge him!

Meeting with God

One time as he was sitting in Moriah chapel listening to the preaching he suddenly felt guilty. He realized that he had done things wrong and he needed God to forgive his sins.

For the first time Evan saw that only God could help him.

After he had prayed to God he felt different inside. God really had forgiven him. "God is so amazing. From now on I'm going to put God first," he promised. And he kept his promise.

Evan would come home from work after twelve hours in the mine. His face and body were covered in black coal dust, so his first task on walking in through the door was to have a bath. Then he would find something to eat before walking a full mile to Moriah Chapel.

In one of these meetings, a man read how Jesus had appeared to his disciples after he had come alive again. The first time Jesus appeared after he had come alive again, all the disciples had been there except for doubting Thomas. Thomas had missed out. "Don't miss out on a single meeting with Jesus, my friends." The man encouraged everyone. His words struck Evan who made sure he went to every single meeting from then on.

When he was in the mine he worked hard, but his thoughts were on God. In the evenings he would go to the Chapel or spend his time studying the Bible at home.

Evan just wanted to meet God more. He went on crusades with his dad and spent all his money on books. One book was written by C.R. Sheldon: "In His Steps: What Would Jesus Do?" As Evan read the title he thought to himself, "Jesus has done so much for me. But what have I done for Jesus?"

He was fifteen years old, and now that he had asked the question, God was ready to give him an answer.

Chapter 3
Early Ministry
★ ★ ★ ★

Evan Preaching

Evan the Schoolteacher

When Evan walked into work one day his boss was waiting to speak with him. Evan had become well known to them and they respected him. He worked hard and he told them what he thought. He wasn't afraid to speak up for others, but he was always polite.

He was just the man they were looking for.

"I've set up a school for the poor children Evan, and I want you to help me."

Evan jumped at the chance. He loved being with the children and teaching them what he knew. When the owner of the mine found out what Evan was doing in his spare time, he asked Evan to teach the children music, math and moral values.

Evan was the perfect teacher. He remembered much of his math from school, he loved the Bible the best moral guide for life and he was very musical. He taught himself how to play the violin, the organ and the piano.

The school was very basic, and met in the offices of the mine, but Evan loved it. He just loved being with the children. In fact, all through his life Evan thought that children were really special.

In 1895, the owner decided it was time to build a proper school nearer to the children's homes. Evan was asked to plan and oversee the new building. The new building was named Pisgah, and soon became a chapel on Sunday as well as a school room for the children in the village.

For the next three years Evan worked hard teaching the children, and working in the Sunday school. Before long Evan was in charge of the whole Sunday school, even though he was so young. At last he felt like he was doing something for God.

Evan saw the lives of the children changing as he encouraged them and taught them. He loved his work in Moriah Chapel and in the Pisgah School.

Life was busy for him as a teenager. He even

spent time learning to write shorthand. He loved to make up poems and songs and was a great writer. He won many competitions for his writing. The children in the school had a very rich education when Evan was around.

But it did not last long. There was a huge explosion in the mine and it would cost too much money to repair it. The mine closed down and Evan was out of a job. He traveled all over to find work, doing whatever he could.

Leaving Home

In the end, he left home to work in a place called Mountain Ash, north of Cardiff. With great sadness he said goodbye to the children in the Pisgah School and the children in the Sunday school at Moriah Chapel.

In Mountain Ash, the other miners saw that he was a good worker who was always willing to help them. They didn't always understand why he didn't want to join in their conversations, but they could see he was a deep thinker. The local chapel soon got to know him too. He was only 20 years old but they asked him to speak to the whole church. They could tell that God was with him.

The next few years were really a time of learning and training for him.

Time to Choose a Career

Evan knew that he didn't want to be a miner for the rest of his life, so he started to look for a different trade. In those days you would go and work for somebody and they would train you to do their job.

Evan's uncle was a blacksmith so Evan asked if he could come and learn to be a blacksmith with him. The family paid his uncle some money and Evan agreed to do three years of training with him. Evan planned to go to America, earn lots of money as a blacksmith then return to Wales to retire.

But God had other plans for him.

It was a Friday night and Evan was walking home with his friend Mr. Morgan. Mr. Morgan was training to be a minister in the church. As they spoke, something began to stir inside Evan. As far back as he could remember Evan had wanted to serve God with all his heart. He had done lots of things, but he still felt like he was not doing enough for God. Now he saw what he could do.

That night Evan decided to become a minister, just like his friend. He was already becoming a very good blacksmith, now he knew that God had a different plan for him.

But Evan still wasn't sure. He had agreed to be with his uncle for three years, but he had only been there for eighteen months. He couldn't just leave. He was torn between pleasing his uncle and obeying God.

At some point in our lives everyone has to

make this kind of decision. When we choose to obey God, He will never let us down. Evan's mom spoke to his uncle and his uncle said Evan was allowed to go on the condition that the uncle was given some money.

Lots of Praying

Evan spoke only about God all the time he was staying with his uncle. At every meal he would sit and read the Bible, and after the meal he would study and read the Bible late into the night.

Evan loved to pray. When he was out walking, sometimes he would stand still and pray with only his lips moving. At night during his prayer time, he would cry out to God for Wales. Sometimes when he prayed he just made groaning sounds. Even as he sat in a room with others, he would be praying quietly. As he worked he would pray. Every moment his thoughts seemed to be on prayer.

Sometimes he was so desperate to talk to God that he didn't want to be around other people, and would go to his room to pray. For hours at a time he would cry out to God. His family would prepare food for him, but he didn't stop to eat it. In fact, he would even forget it was mealtime.

Evan could even be in a conversation with someone and suddenly feel the need to pray. He would stop in the middle of the conversation and go off to his room to pray. Evan was determined to obey the Holy Spirit no matter what other people thought of him.

Evan wanted everyone to love praying like he did. So when Evan realized that some people didn't like to pray in public, he wrote down some prayers for them to say.

One time after Evan had prayed from his heart a local minister came up to him, "My friend you have a lot of talents. God could really use you to preach in pulpits. But you must pray about this. You don't want to waste your talent.

Pray!" And Evan did.

For hours at a time he would cry out to God. "God you know that Wales needs you, but is this what you want *me* to do?" He thought of all the competitions and the writings that he enjoyed doing. He had even thought about becoming a poet. Did God really want him to use his talents for that? He loved his poetry, but he loved God more.

While the family sat around talking, Evan would sit there reading. But whenever they spoke about God, Evan would put down his book and join in the conversation. It was obvious to everyone that God wanted Evan to be a minister.

Chapter 4
Called to the Ministry

★ ★ ★ ★

On fire for God

"I Must Obey the Holy Spirit."

Evan's leaders were worried about him and had said to him, "You pray a lot, then you come home from the church service and you're up half the night talking and praying with a friend." Evan knew they wanted him to explain his actions, but he couldn't. All he knew was that the Spirit moved him and he obeyed. He and his friends always talked about God and prayed for a revival to come to Wales and the world.

When the leaders of the church agreed he could start to train for the ministry. Evan was excited, but something bigger was stirring inside him.

He wrote to Mr. Morgan, "I've prayed that God will baptize you and me with the Holy Spirit."

A few weeks later he was lying in bed and he felt very afraid. He started to shiver all over and the bed began to shake. His brother Dan rushed in from the room next door, thinking that Evan was sick, but soon realized it was the Holy Spirit working in Evan.

The next night Evan woke up at one a.m. and felt he needed to pray for a few hours.

Night after night this went on. Each night he would pray from one a.m. until five a.m. in the morning. Then he would go back to sleep until nine a.m. He would then spend most of the morning praying too.

Something special was happening in those times. Evan was already passionate for God, but now he was being changed by God.

He had been brought up in a godly home; and had chosen to follow God. He had given all his spare time to God, but now God was meeting with him. It was as if every part of him was being changed.

One night he woke up feeling very sad. It seemed like Christianity had failed and was dying, and Evan felt a strong need to pray. By the time morning came, Evan knew that God was about to move, not just in him, but across the land.

Fighting the Inner Battles

Evan knew that God had done something special inside him. He had longed for and prayed for revival. Now God had put revival fire in him. In 1903, he stood up in front of the congregation at Moriah Chapel and said, "I have reached out my hand and touched the flame. I am burning and waiting for a sign."

In the meantime, God continued His work in Evan teaching him how to live life as His child, bringing him through battles and victories to grow his faith and trust in Him. Evan desperately wanted to serve God, but he also felt like he was going to fail God. "God I'll do anything for you," he would pray, but a few days later he would be struggling with sin. Instead of thinking about how God would help him, Evan thought only about how he couldn't help himself.

Sometimes Evan was very excited to be following God, but at other times he was depressed. In all of this battle, though, Evan did not give up on his plans to follow God; in fact it just made him fight harder. God was using this battle that was going on inside Evan to get him ready for the future. Each time he felt like he couldn't fight anymore, Evan found that God still had enough grace to help him. God always gave Evan the grace he needed at the right time.

Meeting Mr. Phillips

Evan was ready to become a minister. After lots more preaching and an exam his leaders agreed that he was ready. They sent him to a college where he could study more about God and the work of the ministry. So on September 13, 1904, Evan began his college training. At college, Evan Roberts met with the older Christian that he needed to be able to guide him through his battles. Mr. Evan Phillips had been part of a revival in Wales back in 1859. Mr. Phillips spent a lot of time praying and asking God to bring a revival to Wales again and often told his congregation to pray and ask God for the same thing.

When Evan preached a sermon everyone noticed that there was something different about it. As he spoke it was like fire was coming out of his mouth and burning the words into their hearts. Mr. Phillips noticed it too. God was clearly with Evan, and Mr. Phillips wondered, could this be one of the people that God was raising up in answer to his prayers?

Mr. Phillips often asked Evan to come to his house and Evan loved to hear stories about the past revival. Evan had many dreams and visions, and some of them were scary and some were exciting. Mr. Phillips was the first man he felt he could share his visions with. Being a wise man, Mr. Phillips knew just what to say.

Some of the dreams were clearly from God. Others clearly were not. Mr. Phillips was wise enough to spot the difference. So when Evan started to share stories of his dreams to see Wales changed, Mr. Phillips knew that God was calling Evan to the task.

"I can see myself helping thousands of people to meet with God and live for Him," Evan shared. Mr. Phillips smiled as he saw his prayers being answered in young Evan.

Mr. Phillips' family enjoyed having Evan in the home. They tried to get him to talk more and managed to get him to smile at their jokes, but they never managed to get him to laugh at them. They also loved listening to the sayings that he made up.

"You can always smile at the world, when God smiles at your soul," he would say and they would break out into a smile.

Focused on Jesus

Evan loved reading. One of his favorite books was by John Bunyan, called Pilgrim's Progress. He also loved to learn about faith. One man, George Müller, fed thousands of orphans every day by faith. All Mr. Müller did was pray and God sent people with food or money. Evan was inspired by the God of Mr. Müller and knew that the same God was with him on his life's journey. After all, the whole focus of Evan's life was on Jesus.

After years of simply gazing at Jesus, and hours spent in prayer and study, Evan knew that God had done something in him. God had been looking for someone who would be looking for Him and Evan was just the man.

Chapter 5
Time to Bend

★ ★ ★ ★

Evan preparing to minister

What if I Fail God?

Sidney Evans came back from a prayer meeting and said, "Evan it was amazing. God was there. I have given my life fully to do God's work."

Evan was not excited when he heard this, instead he started thinking, "What if I don't get everything God has for me?" Then he felt depressed.

His friends tried to cheer him up, but nothing seemed to help.

In one prayer meeting Evan could not even put his prayers into words; it just came out as a cry: "Oh, Oh, Oh!" Just like the prophet Isaiah prayed: "Oh, that you would leave heaven and come down," so Evan's heart was crying out for God with a big loud Oh. (See Isaiah 64:1.).

The next day Evan and his friends were with an evangelist called Seth Joshua. Evan sat still, just like he did in other meetings. It was like he was in a trance. But when Seth started to pray, something happened inside Evan.

"Bend us Lord! Bend us!" Seth cried out. Seth knew that it is easy to do what you want to do, instead of doing what God wants you to do. That's why he was asking God to bend him away from what he wanted and towards what God wanted. This is just what had been worrying Evan, so Evan joined in the prayer.

When Evan and his friends went back to Seth's house for breakfast Evan could not eat. "What if I fail God? What if I don't bend and do what He wants me to do? What if I reject the Holy Spirit?"

Of course Evan shouldn't have been so worried. He should have just trusted God. God was obviously doing something in him and getting him ready. God wasn't trying to trick Evan. God was leading Evan into his destiny! And God never asks us to do something that we can't do. Once He's asked us, He always goes on to help us.

Evan couldn't stay around his friends anymore. He had to go and pray. He knew something was wrong in his heart, because when he thought about the Cross it didn't affect him. Jesus' death on the Cross meant that he could be saved from sin. Surely he should feel something when he thought about it?

"I can cry because my heart is so hard, but I can't cry because of what Jesus did for me."

The Life Giving Spirit

Rushing back to the chapel where they had had the prayer meeting, Evan started to cry out to God. "Bend me! Bend me!"

As he prayed he felt the Holy Spirit sweep into him. It was as if his whole life had been cleaned from the inside out. Tears streamed down his face as he felt God's living energy burst through his body. He knew that God had changed him.

When his friends saw him they could see something different. His face seemed to be glowing and they could feel God's presence in his life. Not only that, but he was no longer shy and he was physically stronger, able to walk long distances without tiring. God had changed his whole life.

Wherever Evan went people felt inspired to pray. Evan could feel God's call weighing on his life more. As he tried to study he found it really hard, his heart wasn't in it. He wanted to be out there reaching out to the lost. The only peace he found was by holding the Bible and he always spent more time praying than he did studying.

Now Evan's faith was growing, "God give me 100,000 souls in Wales I pray." Nobody could doubt that God would probably answer his prayer. After all, they could see that God was with him. All those years of pain and of chasing after God were now beginning to pay off.

Let's Go on a Mission

Evan, Sidney and a couple of their friends decided to go on a mission to a local chapel. "But before we do anything we must ask God for direction," Evan commanded.

The students knelt together. "Oh God we want your direction. Please show us who should go, where you want us to go, when you want us to go and how."

As they waited for an answer Evan heard something that surprised him.

"Evan, you asked me who, where, when and how you should go. But you did not ask me *if* you should go."

God wanted Evan to ask about everything before he made a decision. God wants us to do the same too. Evan and his team had learned a very important lesson.

For the next few weeks they traveled around. Wherever they went people were turning to God.

But not everyone was happy.

"Who do these students think they are? Do they think God has only called them to go out? Anyway that Evan bloke is strange." In a way they were right. God hadn't just called this group of students, but they were the ones that were doing it. It was also true that Evan was different. They were not used to his way of doing things.

Instead of preaching in the pulpit, he would walk up and down the church asking people questions. Sometimes in the middle of a service he would jump and say, "You people are not serious. You're just going through the motions with God. You are not actually worshiping Him!"

In one meeting Evan pointed out, "this service seems to be more about people up front showing off what they can do, instead of people worshiping Jesus." After saying that, he then burst into prayer. It was a typical Evan prayer: one that came out of a heart that was bursting with passion for God and a desire to see every person in the church meet with God.

As one lady led everyone in a song to Jesus, people carried on worshiping, praying and crying for the next two hours. Revival was breaking out, this was the real thing. Finally, people were becoming alive to God and wanted to be with Him.

Back in his room Evan could feel the Holy Spirit so strongly he could hardly stand up. He felt like his soul was going to explode. "That's enough God. Please don't show me anymore of you, I don't think my body can take it."

All through the night he stayed up with Sidney, crying out to God for the lost, weeping at the Cross and praising God for what they had seen.

Time to go Home

The next Sunday Mr. Phillips stood up to preach, "My Bible verse for today is, 'Father, Glorify your Son.'"

Evan's face was shining, "Oh! This place is full of the Holy Spirit. I can feel His presence all around and through me. It's all over me."

All through the day Evan kept praying from that verse, "Glorify your Son. Glorify your Son."

In the evening service, when Mr. Phillips announced his verse Evan lost contact with what was going on around him as God took him on a journey. "Father, the hour is come," Mr. Phillips announced and Evan's body began to shake, his eyes blurred out from his surroundings.

He wasn't listening to Mr. Phillips. Instead he could see a vision of his home church. Moriah Chapel and the Pisgah schoolroom were full of young people. "Go and speak to these people," he heard a voice say. Evan was thinking about this, but the voice kept repeating, "You Must Go!" Finally Evan agreed, "God I will do whatever you want me to do."

At that moment he saw the chapel where he sat fill with light. It was a heavenly light, so bright that he could hardly see Mr. Phillips preaching on the other side of the light. Of course, it could all have been in Evan's imagination. Evan thought he had better check that this vision had come from God. Knocking on Mr. Phillips door that evening, he explained what had happened to him.

Mr. Phillips knew at once that this was God at work. At ten a.m., on Monday October 31, Evan got onto a train to travel home for a week. Some of the students thought he was crazy to leave the college. He didn't even have permission to go.

But soon all of Wales would realize that God had told him to leave. The revival was about to take off.

Chapter 6
Revival Begins
★ ★ ★ ★

Evan Preaches

Hi Mom, I'm Home.

When Evan walked into his house his family was surprised to see him.

"We thought you were studying at college. What are you doing here?"

When Evan told them why he had come they were a little worried. They could see there was something different about him, but they couldn't see what God had called him to do.

He was acting strange. He sat in a corner laughing, "This place will be so different in two weeks' time." He started to sing a song to God but ended up crying.

They couldn't understand what he meant by all this. Was he going crazy? They were about to find out.

Evan's brother Dan sat around the table at home. God had been doing something in him and he had started to pray for revival too. But for some reason he was going blind. He had to stop work and his future did not look good.

Evan turned to his brother and said, "Dan, you will not be blind, you shall see. God needs you."

When Dan went back to the specialist he could see. His family realized that God had given Evan a new authority.

The First Week of Meetings

Evan went to the prayer meeting at Moriah Chapel that night. After the meeting he invited the young people to stay and pray some more with him. Sixteen adults and one girl stayed behind.

Evan prayed and encouraged them to stand up and say that Jesus was their God. After two hours everybody had stood. It was a strange meeting and got people talking. Those who had been there thought it was very unusual, but they left feeling different that Monday evening.

The next night Evan held a meeting at Pisgah School. More people came along.

"You must confess that Jesus is your God, be filled with the Holy Spirit and get rid of everything that God does not want you to do." Evan told them.

When he sat down, people who had been at the meeting the night before stood up and shared their story. "We did this last night and now we feel very different."

After three hours, six more people had stood to their feet to confess Christ.

The next day Evan went to a village close by. He met with some people in the local pastor's home and told them what God had been doing. They followed him back to Moriah Chapel for the evening meeting.

It was a hard meeting. Some people didn't believe that God had sent Evan, but some stood up to say that Jesus Christ was their Lord. Getting the Christians to admit in public that they were following Jesus was a key part of what was going to happen in the future.

Evan went to the meeting on Thursday. The minister was late and Evan was asked to be the leader. Afterwards Evan met with the young people, and ten people stood to confess Christ.

"Make another ten stand up Lord," Evan prayed. Slowly ten more people stood before the meeting came to an end at ten p.m. By Friday night the whole village was talking about these strange meetings. People from different churches came to find out more.

Evan encouraged everyone to follow God, confess Christ, obey the Holy Spirit, and do nothing bad. "Now anyone who wants to speak can." With that he sat down.

People started to sing songs to God; someone else prayed; others confessed their sins. Then people gave testimonies and there was more singing. People began to realize that God was working in their midst and the time just seemed to fly by. In fact, it was half past eleven before the meeting came to an end.

Here Come the People

As Evan went to the chapel on Saturday

evening he had no idea what he was going to say. But then God gave him a verse: "Don't be drunk with wine, but be filled with the Holy Spirit." Evan told them how alcohol was ruining families and the community. (See Ephesians 5:18.).

More people were at the meeting, more people took part in it. It was no longer just young people but people of all ages were coming to the meeting and it seemed like everyone wanted more of God. The meeting started at seven, but went on until half past midnight.

At Sunday evening's meeting there were even more people. God was leading people to come. "We must obey the Holy Spirit," Evan taught them. And then he led them in a prayer, "Send the Holy Spirit now, for Jesus Christ's sake."

One week into the revival and everyone was praying for more of God. Something amazing had happened in this sleepy village. Revival was breaking out.

The next Monday the prayer meeting was full. It had never been that way before. When Evan arrived at eight, to lead the evening meeting after the prayer meeting, everyone was ready. "You must confess Christ. Stand up and say He is your God." People started to stand, nearly everyone was crying. If anyone didn't want to stand up, everyone else started to pray for them.

A loud noise filled the room as people started to feel God's presence like they never had before. People fell to the floor crying out to God.

"Send the Holy Spirit now, for Jesus Christ's sake," Evan prayed. Then everyone started to pray. But before they could say it a second time some started to groan in agony. "My sins are too great. Pray for me!" they shouted.

People could not hold back anymore. Their prayers were not tame, but wild. They were not quiet or formal, but they were the prayers of desperate people, asking God to forgive them.

Some just sat and sobbed as the Holy Spirit came and touched them.

Without being asked, different people began to lead the whole congregation in songs and prayers, shouting out worship to God. At three in the morning the meeting ended seven hours after it had begun.

Evan, His Mom, and the Revival

On Tuesday the chapel was full to overflowing. People expected God to come again, but He didn't come in the same way. They kept praying and sometimes they felt God come closer, but not like the last night. By three in the morning many people went home, even Evan's mother got up to leave.

"Please stay mom, the Holy Spirit is about to come," Evan pleaded. But she didn't listen. When she got home she couldn't sleep.

Now only the young people were left. Evan called them all into the middle of the room and as they started to pray, God's power came into the room. Once more people were overwhelmed by the Holy Spirit and worshiped God with tears of repentance and of joy. They finally left for home at six in the morning.

As Evan lay sleeping in his bed he suddenly heard his mother shouting from downstairs, "I'm dying, help me. I'm dying."

He ran downstairs and saw that she wasn't dying from illness; instead God had allowed her to see how awful her sins were. She needed God. Evan prayed with her until she found God's peace.

Revival had come to Evan's home and his local village, and now other people wanted him to bring God to where they were. Evan knew that he could not do all the work on his own. He sent a message to his college. "We need help, please send people quickly."

Chapter 7
Revival Spreads
★ ★ ★ ★

A revival meeting

The Next Village is Touched

For just over a week Evan had been working in his home village. Now the Holy Spirit wanted him to take the revival elsewhere. First of all he went to a small village called Brynteg. By the second night so many people were coming that they had to move to a different building. People ran straight from work, skipping supper, in case there would not be room for them in the chapel.

Emotions were high as people poured out their hearts to God and Evan marched up and down the aisles of the church, praying and waving his Bible in a beckoning manner as if to draw people in. People started coming from further away, having heard about the strange things that were taking place.

One elderly man stood to his feet to speak and motioning toward Evan said, "Many people have said that this man is going crazy. But I need to tell you that back in the revival of 1859 there were many people just like him. You don't need to be afraid; you just need to obey God."

Evan burst out laughing, God was breaking through and tearing down every concern that people had. Now God had broken down all the barriers to do whatever He wanted to do.

When God wants to do something, He looks for people He can work through and then He makes everything else happen. So God's biggest concern is for our hearts to be ready for Him, He does the rest.

The Papers Tell the News

The Western Mail Newspaper carried a report of the revival on Thursday, September 10:

"An amazing revival is happening in Loughor. Evan Roberts is leading the people to God. His words stir people up to believe in God again. Shopkeepers are closing their shops early to get to the meetings and miners are coming straight from work to be there. The meetings go on until the middle of the night.

Everyone there is talking about what is happening as churches and ministers from all backgrounds come together."

Now people were reading about the revival in their homes. People who had come to a meeting were going back to their churches to hold meetings. They wrote to Evan to tell him about it.

"Dear Mr. Roberts, since we were in your meeting we have felt different. We have found it so much easier to pray. We went home and started revival meetings, and would love for you to come to them. We know that they would be so much stronger if you were here."

Moriah Chapel was now too small to hold the revival. The reporters could not understand it, there were no special singers and no advertising, but over 650 people were filling the largest building in the village.

In a Revival Meeting

People knelt, unable to stand, unable to talk because their minds were full of how they had let God down. They cried out to God in their hearts for Him to forgive them. People went to those who were kneeling to pray for them.

Some stood to pray but fell down on the floor because the powerful presence of God in the room was too much for their physical bodies to cope with.

"Lord save the drunks. Let them know you." A voice rang out in prayer.

Others were groaning as they agreed with the prayer. Their minds were so full of God that their hearts were bursting for the things that He wanted to see.

A few weren't happy: "Why does Evan Roberts let whoever wants to, just go ahead and pray? It can't be right. These meetings are chaos." Thankfully God didn't listen to them. God wants to meet with ordinary people and work through ordinary people.

The meeting went on until five in the morning. Afterwards Evan met with a few people.

"If people are upset because of their sin, put one hand on their shoulder and hold their other hand. Pray for them; then ask them if *they* want to pray and ask for forgiveness. If they do want to, help them to know how to pray and lead them to thank God."

When these instructions were followed the next night, people's faces glowed as they were helped to find God.

The People Tell the News

People in the village were desperate for more of God. "Save my friend, save my family. Oh God, please come now. Send the Spirit." Prayer meetings were held in houses throughout the day. People couldn't keep God to themselves. They started to tell people about Him wherever they went.

The next day, people who had not spoken to each other for years became friends again. Others who had read the newspaper article traveled to Loughor to be part of the revival. Evan's friend, Sidney, also came to join what God was doing.

A long time before the start of the meeting, Moriah Chapel was full. "Open up the old chapel, Sidney will lead a meeting there for anyone who can't fit in here," Evan said. Within minutes the old chapel was full too.

Revival hymns were being sung: "Here is Love, Vast As The Ocean", and "Throw Out A Lifeline" were to become firm favorites in the revival. The first song was about God's amazing love in forgiving us, the second invited people to be saved by Jesus Christ.

Two weeks after the first meeting, the place was on fire for Jesus. People, who had thought that Evan was crazy before, were now as crazy for Jesus as he was.

Evan was getting invitations from many places. But he had decided only to go where

God told him to. Then he received an invitation from the pastor of a church, "please come," and he knew God wanted him to go.

Moving Villages

He took some girls with him to help with the music at the start the service. In the first meeting a girl started to sing but then burst into tears. Another girl did the same. The congregation was puzzled. They had invited Evan Roberts to come but he was not speaking.

Then a lady fell to her knees and started to confess her sins. People were shocked; then they were convicted. Before long everyone was mourning their sins and crying out to God. Then they were shouting out in praise as God forgave them.

Song after song was sung. People forgot to go home for Sunday lunch. God was in the house. The evening service became one long prayer meeting.

The next morning everyone was talking about what God had done. That evening people began to gather for the service. However, when the service started there were only a few people because many of those who came after work went home first to wash of the day's dirt. Bit by bit they all came in.

Evan was very excited about the service as he walked up and down the aisle, swinging his arms, and greeting each person who came in with a big smile.

People walked home from that evening service talking about God.

As Evan said, "Religion should be the happiest thing in life, not boring or gloomy. Would a father be upset if his child laughs? Of course not! Well we are in Daddy God's house, we should be laughing and happy…God will not be upset."

Evan wasn't like the other preachers. He didn't

shout. He didn't bang his fist on the pulpit. He just smiled and spoke normally. As he spoke you could feel that he loved the people, and his words changed their lives, because he was speaking what the Holy Spirit told him to say.

For the next few months Evan traveled all around the South of Wales and wherever he went God was with him. The presence of God was also in lots of places where Evan had not been, for those who had been at the meetings took the presence of God with them when they went home, to work, and wherever they went.

God's presence was also felt in places where nobody had ever met Evan. In fact, Evan was nowhere near around 80% of the places where the revival broke out. God's presence was flowing wherever He wanted it to go because this was not Evan Robert's revival, this was God reviving His church and changing the nation.

Chapter 8
Revival Fruits
★ ★ ★ ★

Cymanfa y Presbyteriaid

Gathering to hear the word in Wales

Salvation Changes People

People were meeting with God. They could not keep it to themselves. Everywhere they went they would talk about Him. People who were avoiding the revival meetings could not avoid the revival. Everyone was talking about it.

A policeman came to a meeting to find out what was going on and found God. That night he was saved.

The reporter of the Western mail came up to Evan for an interview, "What shall I write in the paper about this?" But Evan did not answer. Instead he prayed, "Lord save the reporter." And the reporter was saved.

The ordinary believer was rising up to serve God. "It's time for each person to take off their jacket and get to work for God's Kingdom," Evan said challenging them.

One miner who was listening stood up and threw off his jacket, "I'm ready to work!"

So many people were being saved that they had to have baptism services. In one church service, ninety-two new believers were baptized.

God was touching people from every part of society and some of the biggest changes took place hundreds of feet underground in the coal mines.

Revival Down the Mines

Down in the mines people would sing praise to God. Prayer meetings took place underground and over half of the miners would go to pray during their lunch break. The work was disrupted by the revival, but people were working so much harder that no one noticed.

Some miners went to work one hour earlier so that they could pray together before they started work. Even the miners who were not saved had to change. Their friends were different and that affected them too.

One of the mine managers was a leader in his church. But when he saw how his miners were changed he realized that he wasn't saved. His workers knelt around him and prayed for him as he gave his life to Christ. These were strange and wonderful days for everyone.

Before the miners were saved, many of them used to swear; now hardly anyone did. In fact, even the donkeys in the mines were confused. The donkeys were used to carrying the coal to the surface. They were used to being kicked and sworn at to get them to go. When the revival came they couldn't understand the new and gentler treatment they were getting. The people whose job was to take care of the donkeys were worried about their jobs, because the miners were taking such good care of the donkeys that they didn't have any work to do.

The effects of the revival lasted for many years. Before the revival, people would go on strike, refusing to work until they were paid more. After the revival it was a long time before anyone went on strike. Everyone knew God had done something special.

In one mine the ropes of the lift broke.

The miners were stuck underground. With nowhere to go and nothing to do, one of the men suggested they should hold a prayer meeting to pass the time. Everyone agreed, even though many of them were not saved. As they sang and prayed several hours went by.

One man became very convicted of his sins and tried to find a place to hide himself away from the presence of God. Many of the miners accepted Christ there and when they finally climbed out everyone knew that they would remember that time for the rest of their lives.

Sick with Sin

Mrs. Powell was a respectable lady. She had been going to church for 35 years, taught in the Sunday school and looked after people who were sick. Everyone thought she was a good lady. Even she thought she was, until the revival came.

Mrs. Powell didn't approve of the revival.

"Everyone is so noisy, it's not right," she said, "and the women should not be speaking in the church. And they shouldn't be staying up so late, they will be tired the next day."

Mrs. Powell didn't go to the Sunday service. This caused quite a stir among the congregation, and rumors started going around that she had gone mad. Some of those in the congregation felt they should go and visit her. "It's not like you to miss church. You are one of the most devoted Christians," they said encouragingly.

"I am not a Christian; I've only been pretending all these years," she replied.

The people couldn't believe it! For two weeks she did not eat or drink, but lay in her bed moaning all day long because of her sin. The doctors did not know how to help her. She seemed to have lost her mind. When her bed started to shake one day they went running up to check on her. "You must rest," they said. But she refused. She was jumping around the room praising God and her face was glowing.

The next day she was in the chapel and when there was a chance during the service for people to come to the front to tell what God had done for them, she was the first to go. "Some of you have heard that I went crazy, and you were right. I realized after all of these years of pretending to follow Jesus that it was all a lie. I was full of lies. A month ago I saw what I was really like for the first time."

"Before then I thought I had kept all of the Ten Commandments, but suddenly I realized I had broken every single one of them lots of times. I was so full of sin that I didn't think I could be forgiven. For the last two weeks all I have seen is my sin, like huge mountains around me, covered in mist and darkness."

"One morning I cried out to God, 'I know I deserve hell, and I am ready to go, but before you send me there please let me see the Man who died for me.' At that moment the mist cleared and a bright light filled the whole room. I closed my eyes tightly and tried to ready myself to die and go to hell as the mountains of sin filled my mind...suddenly, I opened my eyes and the mountains of sin were gone...Jesus had forgiven me, Jesus' blood had cleansed me and set me free!

"My mountains of sin have been taken away. Jesus' blood has set me free. My doctor asked me to be quiet, but how can I be quiet. Jesus has forgiven me! I am free. I have been saved from hell. Praise God. Thank you God!"

As Mrs. Powell sat back down, a great silence filled the room as the Spirit of God hovered over the people for thirty minutes or more... then one by one the people began to slip away to their homes in awe of what God had done.

You've probably realized by now that a revival can be very noisy or it can be very quiet. In fact, the only thing you could be sure of was that you did not know what to expect when the presence of God filled the meeting place. In one meeting, everyone sat in silence for two hours, for the presence of God so filled the room they could not even speak

When people left the revival meetings they did not leave the revival. They took it with them. As people left the meetings they sang to God on their way home. Day and night songs of praise and worship could be heard across the nation coming from homes and the streets of the towns. In the shops the people gladly shared the Gospel, and in the workplaces they sang hymns of praise.

Not everyone agreed with the revival, but even the toughest rebel could not avoid it!

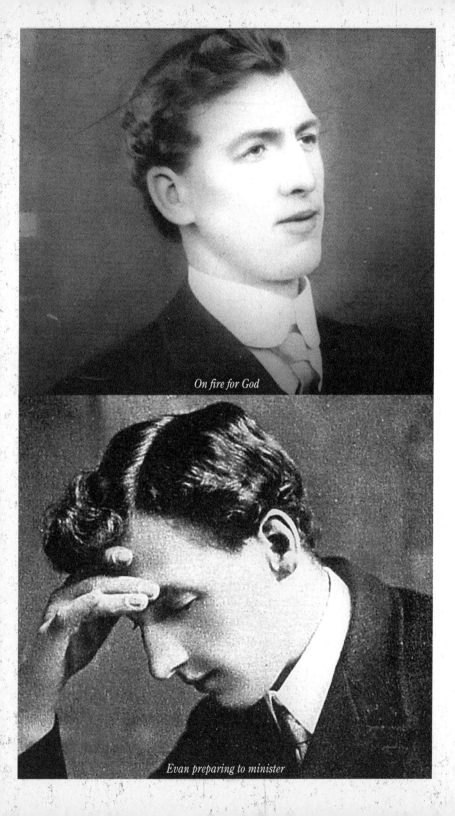

On fire for God

Evan preparing to minister

Evan preparing to minister

An older Evan Roberts

Moriah Chapel

Mr. and Mrs. Penn-Lewis

Chapter 9
Rebels Saved

★ ★ ★ ★

Evan Preaching

Reaching Out to the Bars

Lots of people went out onto the streets to tell people about Jesus, but not everyone wanted to listen to them. Some people shouted at the

Christians, but the Christians did not give up. Before long many more people were coming to know Jesus. God's Church had come alive and now it was doing God's work.

Some people held meetings on the streets. In one meeting a drunken man started to insult the Christians…and in reply the Christians prayed for him and he was soon saved. In the bars, people left their drinks on the tables and went to the meetings. When the meetings ended, those who had been in the bars didn't go back to the bars to finish their drinks. They had found something much better; they had found Jesus.

When the bars closed at 1:30 each morning the Christians were ready and waiting outside to sing songs of praise to God. Oftentimes a policeman would tell them to stop singing even though he didn't really want them to, but the owners of the bars would complain against the Christians because their singing caused many of the customers of the bars to be saved and stop going to the bars.

For the next few days the Christians who sang outside the bars found that God didn't help them like He had before. They had let God down by turning away from those in the bars. The group repented and went back to singing outside the bars at closing time. The bar owners were scared because more and more people were getting saved. People were spending all their time in church, and nobody was drinking.

Sometimes when people went singing outside the bars, those who didn't want to hear them would escape out the back way to avoid the revivalists. Those who didn't escape would end up being saved.

Just as Jesus did, the Christians went wherever the worst sinners were. Some went to the worst parts of town and the poorest homes where people lived in slums. Others met with the homeless. Passersby would look on as a homeless man knelt next to a smartly dressed lady in the middle of the street. As they knelt together in prayer, tears would spill down his face as he gave his life to Jesus.

Lord, Make me a Missionary

One shy man woke up in the middle of the night feeling like he had to pray. As he prayed and cried for hours he saw Jesus on the Cross. That night he decided to be a missionary for Jesus.

When he got up the next day he slipped his Bible into his pocket. Before he got to work two of the burliest and most dangerous men were waiting for him. But they didn't want to cause him any trouble, instead they asked him to hold a prayer meeting. "Let's meet at lunchtime to pray," he said.

When that lunch time arrived, he and the two men met together, they read the Bible feeding on Christ Jesus, the Bread of Life, then they prayed and the new missionary led one of the greatest rebels in his workplace to Jesus.

An Atheist Believes in God

Tom was a member of the Ethical Society, a society for atheists, who do not believe in God. Tom loved to sing, so when he passed a chapel and heard the most beautiful singing he had ever heard, he wanted to listen to it some more. He went back the next night and something changed inside him.

Rushing home he got hold of all his anti-God books and threw them into the fire. "Tom, what's the matter. You've gone mad! You'll burn the whole house down." his wife said.

"No, quite the opposite! God has kept us safe all these years even though these books were in the house, He will continue to keep us safe now that these books are going."

"Now I am going to the chapel to give my life to Christ." He announced to his wife.

"Tom! Don't do it. Be reasonable, let's sing instead." She begged.

Tom stayed to sing, but when he went to work people could see he had changed.

One of the other Christian workers spoke to him, "You know Tom, the doors of the chapel are always wide open to you. You are welcome to join us."

Tom smiled, "If the doors were closed I would climb in through the window. If the windows were locked I would get a ladder, climb on to the roof and break in. You can't stop me from being there!" The God, whom Tom didn't even believe in before, had now got hold of him.

Mockers Become Converts

Four travelers sat in a bar, mocking the revival.

An older man was listening in and could take it no more. "This is God's work. You shouldn't make fun of it."

But the men just laughed at him.

When the older man had finished his writings he approached the men again. "There's a meeting tonight at the chapel. You should come with me."

One of the travelers looked up, "You know what, I feel bored tonight. This sounds like fun."

As they walked into the meeting it had already started and a man was in the middle of a prayer, "Lord, bless someone here tonight. It may be that person has just walked in, but he is an enemy of yours." A lady then started singing, "Tell Mother I'll Be There."[1]

As she sang the traveler turned pale, "My mother died brokenhearted because of me. Nobody will be able to tell her that I'll be there. I am the greatest sinner of all. What can I do? Please help me!"

---

1 A Hymn written in 1898 by Charles Fillmore

With sobs and tears he gave his life to Jesus. Many years later he told his story. By that time he was an elder in his church and his three traveling friends had come to know Jesus too.

One Word: Aceldama

In one meeting there were no testimonies, only prayer. After two and a half hours one lady stood and said, "We have prayed for many hours for God's presence and God has answered, He is here. Now let's forget about ourselves and pray for those who don't know Jesus out there. Let's pray for one person each and stay here, waiting for the answer."

Within seconds everyone was praying for the lost. The lady just kept repeating one word, "Aceldama."

At some point two or three people came into the chapel. The praying went on for over an hour and then there was silence.

A new voice now spoke out, "Lord forgive

me. Help me tell the truth." A lady was walking to the front.

"You know me as Harriet Harris, but really I am Hannah Harris," she told everyone. "I lied to get hold of a farm and some money. I then went back to America and tried to use the money, but everywhere I went I kept hearing the word 'Aceldama'—the field of blood. I knew I had to find my sister somewhere in America."

"America is a big place but at last I found my sister. She is here tonight, but I am a thief who was willing to steal from my sister. Only that word Aceldama got in my way. The field I stole was like a field full of blood because I had stolen it."

By the time Hannah left she knew that God and her sister had forgiven her.

God Points Out the Lost

Gamblers were saved, drunks became sober and were set free, bullies found that Jesus still loved them and were freed from their lives of terror. In some places whole crowds of rebels were saved, crying out to God.

Sometimes when Evan was preaching he would stop, "There is someone up in the balcony that needs help," everyone would turn to see a man in need, nobody else had noticed him, but the Holy Spirit had pointed him out.

At other times Evan would leap up, "There is someone outside right now who needs Jesus, quickly someone go and help them." On leaving the chapel they would find a lady crumpled under the conviction of God or a man with tears streaming down his face. They would be brought into the meeting and brought to Jesus.

God was showing Evan these people even though he couldn't see them with his natural eyes. God was seeking out those who were lost.

So many people were turning away from their sins and being saved that the whole of society was changing. The police had very little to do. In some parts of Wales the courts were empty and the judges had no work. Nobody was committing crime!

God's revival was touching the rich and the poor, those brought up in church and those who had never even seen a Bible. The young people and the elderly were all serving God. And as with any revival the children were a big part of it.

Chapter 10
The Children

★ ★ ★ ★

Evan — a man of study prayer

A Part of the Meetings

Imagine if these things happened where you live. What kind of difference would it make where you live if everyone was talking about

God and half the people were saved? What would you do?

I'll tell you what Jesus did, He told the people to let the children come to Him, He loved them and when He was ministering to the people, He wanted the children to listen and learn too. Evan Roberts loved children too, and wanted them in his meetings. So, the children in Wales were right in the middle of the revival. They weren't just watching it happen, they were part of it. In fact, Evan expected them to be a part of it. The children received the Holy Spirit and took part in the meetings just like the adults did.

Right from the first week of the revival he taught the children to pray: "Send the Spirit for Jesus Christ's sake." And the children prayed it in the morning and at night.

During the meetings if the children had something to say, they were allowed to share it with everyone. In one meeting the children started singing a praise song to God. Some of the adults tried to get the children to be quiet, so the *proper* meeting could begin, but Evan leapt to his feet and said, "Jesus said, 'let the children come to me and do not hinder them', so let the children sing to Jesus and don't stop them!" (See Matthew 19:14.)

Wherever Evan went he would stop to talk with the children. He loved to share Jesus with them and to listen to them, and they loved to be around him.

Once, when Evan was walking along, he saw some children smoking. He stopped to talk with them and told them how the smoke could damage their bodies. They gave him their cigarettes. Then Evan encouraged them to learn Bible verses from memory, because as he said to them, "Now is the best time for you to do it!"

As the children left, Evan thanked each one of them for the way they had shared together. The children left knowing that they were special to Evan and more importantly they knew they were special to God.

Children Leading Revival

In one church the children met together for their regular Sunday school lesson but it turned into a prayer meeting instead. As they prayed, they cried out to God from their hearts. For three hours the children prayed as if they were adults, using the Bible in their prayers. Tears poured down their faces as they cried out to God for the lost.

When the adults saw what was going on they left what they were doing and joined in with the children's group.

In another class the children started to sing praise to God. As they sang the Holy Spirit inspired their song and they marched around the room. Before long they had marched to where the adults were meeting. Soon everyone was praising God together, as the spirit of revival touched the adults.

Of course their revival was not only in the church. Children could be found praying all over the school playgrounds. Even children as young as three were praying and talking about the power of God in the revival.

And the children didn't just talk about the revival; they lived it. They didn't just worship God; they lived for Him and worked for Him. Hundreds of children led their parents to Christ at home. Other children held open air meetings, inviting their friends to follow Jesus.

Remember this revival was all about God working and God can work through anyone no matter how young they are. The key is to connect with Him and these children were doing that as they prayed and worshipped Him with all their heart.

From Gang to God

Dafydd (pronounced David) Jones was 13 when the revival started. Dafydd had a very hard life. His mom had died when he was young and his dad was a drunk. His grandmother looked after him, but Dafydd was very angry inside. He had started to get involved with the local gangs, causing trouble.

Dafydd's grandmother went to church often and always prayed for him. When the revival came she was very excited.

One day Dafydd went to her chapel with his grandmother. She stood up and read from the Bible. Then she started to explain what it meant. Dafydd felt the whole building shaking. As he looked around he realized that it wasn't the building, it was his body!

Some ladies started to sing and he could feel God in that place. The Holy Spirit's power was working mightily in him. When he got home he told another boy what had happened. As he shared with the boy, both of them were filled with the Holy Spirit at home. They then started to pray for his dad.

Before long his dad was saved and set free from alcohol. His dad became a Sunday school leader. Dafydd was different too. He no longer wanted to be part of a street gang; he had decided to join God's gang. When the revival came to an end Dafydd forgot about God for a few years, but he soon came back to God and traveled around Wales preaching the Gospel. He continued preaching until he was 96 years old!

God Loves Families

Whole families were changed by the revival. As parents came to know Jesus they were changed. Some children who had horrible lives at home found that their home suddenly became a place of safety and laughter. In fact, the social workers who helped families with problems found that they didn't have any work to do during the revival because so many families were being changed by God.

God just loves to touch families. One Sunday a farmer came into the church. He was a large man with big strong hands. But this day he had tears in his eyes. He walked to the front and knelt next to the pulpit. As he knelt to pray, everyone in the church became quiet.

The farmer started to cry out to God. Everyone knew this farmer was a sinner because of the evil things he did. Now he was desperate for God to forgive him. As he prayed the preacher stood by in the pulpit, suddenly it looked like a bolt of electricity had hit the preacher; his whole body was shaking. Finally, the preacher knelt beside the farmer and joined in the prayer with him. Their prayer was like a duet to the rest of the church as they listened in.

When the farmer stood he knew he had been forgiven. Looking over at the preacher, he saw that it was his son. The two men hugged each other; father and son were ready to serve God together.

When God moves there is nothing that He cannot do.

Chapter 11
More Revivals

★ ★ ★ ★

Evan Preaching

Evan went on several missionary trips around Wales. Wherever he went God seemed to use him to start a revival, as he moved on the revival continued where he had been.

In each place Evan tried to listen to the Holy Spirit and obey Him. In one place different soloists kept standing up to sing. In the end Evan stood to stop them. "Each one of you is singing to show how well you can sing, instead of singing to praise God. You are blocking the Holy Spirit."

Tired

Evan prayed for long periods of time, whether he was in a meeting, travelling or sitting at home. In the first two months of the revival he hardly took time to eat. And he only slept two or three hours each night. Some of his friends were worried about him.

"Evan you are going to exhaust yourself if you are not careful. You must be tired."

"Tired?" Evan replied. "Not once. God has made me strong. My body is full of electricity day and night and I have no sleep before I am back in meetings again."

But he was forgetting that God planned for our bodies to rest. When God is using us we still need fresh air, food, and rest. If we look after our bodies they will be able to serve God for longer.

The more people suggested he needed to rest, the more impatient and cross he got. He felt he had to keep going, after all God was using him and there was a lot of work to do. So many people wanted to know God. So many places were calling him to come and preach.

Evan was obedient and dependent on the Holy Spirit as he went places. If he felt the Spirit did not want him to preach he would happily sit through a whole service saying nothing, or only praying. He was not going to speak just because people expected him to. In some places he would speak for a couple of hours, in others for only 15 minutes. In each place he asked God what He wanted him to do and tried to obey.

Everywhere he went Evan continued to

challenge people: Who will stand up for Christ? Who will say that Jesus is their God?

The World Joins In

Wherever Evan went the newspapers reported what he had done. As the word spread people started to travel from across Wales. Then people came from England, France, Germany and across Europe. They came from America and Canada. They came from India, China and Africa.

Wherever they came from they came to meet with God. They traveled for months by boat and train to see with their own eyes what God was doing in Wales.

The people of Wales gladly opened their homes up to the travelers to give them somewhere to rest. In each meeting people knew that if they did not get there early they may not get in to the building at all. Most of the people of the town would want to be at a meeting, together with all those who had traveled from outside the town.

Evan was quick to point out where people were hindering the Holy Spirit by not taking part in the service. In one meeting people were singing more and more songs, but they weren't actually worshiping God.

"Stop! Stop, Please!" Evan called out loudly.

When the singer stopped, Evan explained to the people, "In the past I let meetings continue, but now I can't. We are hindering the Holy Spirit from working by the way we are singing this song. I know, and you know, when someone who is singing a song has not been anointed by the Holy Spirit."

Evan didn't want people to come out of curiosity. He didn't want them to come and watch him, but to come and meet with God. If he felt people were there just to look out of curiosity he would stop the service.

While Evan was busy serving God, other ministers were also traveling around spreading the revival. God's work continued to change the lives of individual people, families and whole villages.

Evan was getting so many letters and so many people asking him to come that he had to get a secretary to help him. His secretary helped him organize his travel plans.

In one place, Evan went to the pit of a coal mine early in the morning. Some of the miners had been working all night and Evan shook each one of them by hand. "Good morning, come to the prayer meeting." He smiled so sweetly at them that many of them came. As they stood before God they prayed and wept like babies. God was touching these tough miners.

Evan's whole body was tired, but God kept Evan and the meetings going on. After three weeks of nonstop meetings on one journey he could hardly talk. But as weak as his voice was the people heard him and they began to cry and call out to God. In each meeting people were being saved. In one village over 600 people had been saved in just two weeks!

Supernatural God

Not only were people saved but God was doing miracles in their lives. In one church a boy stood up and said, "ppppppplease pppray fffor mmmmme." He stuttered. The whole church prayed. Then the boy spoke, "God has healed me." For the first time in his life he could speak clearly without stuttering.

In another church there was a man who could not read. He would stand to his feet and recite Scripture. "How do you know so much of the Bible if you can't read?" his friends asked him. "At night time when I can't sleep the Holy Spirit teaches me the verses."

Many people, who were too shy to talk before, became bold when the Holy Spirit filled them with the power of God.

This is what Jesus said would happen in Acts

1:8, "But you shall receive power when the Holy Spirit has come upon you; and you shall be witnesses to Me in Jerusalem, and in all Judea and Samaria, and to the end of the earth." (NKJ)

This is exactly what was happening! People were becoming bold with God's power and witnessing about Him at home. Then they traveled further and further to England, Scotland and the rest of the world to tell people about Jesus. The Holy Spirit was helping people to be Jesus' witnesses.

Not everyone understood that the Holy Spirit could speak to Evan directly. Some of them were confused when he seemed to know where people were sitting who needed Jesus, even though they were not showing any signs of their need.

In one place Evan stopped the meeting and said, "Someone is trying to hypnotize me, to control me." People thought Evan was just imagining things. But then a man stood up and admitted to everyone that he was a hypnotist. Evan had been right.

When you walk close to God it's no surprise that He tells you things that you couldn't know. It's also no surprise that those who don't know God find that hard to understand. Time after time, Evan spoke out what God was telling him.

The reporters watched everything he did and reported everything about the revival in the newspapers.

Chapter 12
The Cost of the Revival
★ ★ ★ ★

EVAN ROBERTS' last Revival Meeting in Anglesey.
LLANFAIRPWLLGWYNGYLLGOGERYCHWYRNDROBWLL-LLANTYSILIOGOGOGOCH.
JULY, 4TH, 1905

The last revival meeting

Feeling Weary

Evan was used to the fact that some people thought he was strange. He didn't mind. But the revival was costing him everything. Because he did not rest, his body could not keep up with his spirit. Evan always admitted that when he thought God was speaking to him, he had to be careful it was not his own imagination, and as his tiredness increased it was harder for him to tell.

One day Evan spoke to his friend, Sidney Evans. "Sidney I was in a meeting recently and I heard a voice telling me to shout: 'Cry out the word Judgment! Judgment!' Thankfully I didn't listen as it was me talking, not the Holy Spirit."

As Evan continued traveling his weariness increased, and he began to speak sharply at some of the meeting saying things like: "How can you come here and sing the song "I Need Thee Every Hour," when you only come to church once a year. You are a bunch of hypocrites." When a toddler gets tired they throw more tantrums, when adults get tired they become very grumpy. The softly spoken Evan was becoming overtired.

When he arrived in a place called Briton Ferry everyone was looking forward to hearing him speak. They gathered for the first meeting, but there was no sign of Evan. After a while his secretary came with a note from him.

"Tell the people that I am not coming to the service. The Holy Spirit stops me from coming. I must pray here for salvation of souls. The Spirit stops me from coming and from speaking."

Everyone was disappointed. His enemies laughed at him and his friends wondered if God would really have spoken to him at the last minute to stop him from going.

Seven Days of Silence and Then More Silence

His hosts also received a note. *"Thank you so much for letting me stay in your house. I am sorry but the Holy Spirit tells me I am not to speak to you. I will be here for seven days and I will speak to no one. Thank you again for letting me be here, I know you will be praying for me."*

And so, for seven whole days nobody heard anything from Evan Roberts. Lots of people were talking about him.

One minister wrote horrible things about Evan

and it really affected him. Evan started to feel troubled like he had in the past, but he did not know how to stop doing God's work. He should have spoken to wiser leaders, but instead he chose to ignore his feelings and carry on.

He took a few more meetings but he was too tired to continue. One evening he simply collapsed from complete exhaustion. He went to stay with a friend and canceled all his meetings. But the people were offended. They put pressure on him until he agreed to run the meeting at a different time. When he arrived he was still exhausted. He rebuked the crowd and as people came and left the meeting he pointed them out as "obstacles arriving" and "obstacles departing." As he spoke, people weren't looking to God; they were looking to see who Evan was talking about.

From all over Wales, people started to criticize him. Evan had no energy left to cope with this and began to condemn whole congregations of people where only one or two did not want

God. He even stopped people from praying for a man, condemning his 'soul' to hell. Of course, Evan could not do that, only God can judge souls, but Evan was exhausted. It wasn't long before he had another breakdown and could not carry on. Once again he was silent.

While he was resting, people kept asking him to come to their churches. He did not feel he could rest for long. He accepted some invitations and the newspapers reported where he would be and when. On the day of the first meeting he did not show up. Instead he spent more time resting and praying.

I Cannot Go On

Now with a more rested body Evan went back to ministry and God started to move as before.

But his body had not fully recovered. In one church, he told them their faith was not built on Jesus. Then when he was asked to speak, he refused to. Instead, he sat in silence for two hours. As people started to complain he stood up and walked out. That evening Evan went back to the same church and spoke freely.

Evan's energy levels were so low that when he heard bad news it made him feel depressed. If he heard about one of the converts falling away from God he would be depressed. The depression caused him to see and hear only the bad things, not the thousands of converts from his ministry that were still living for God.

In between all these breaks, Evan traveled through North Wales and even to Liverpool. Evan had asked God to give him 100,000 souls before the revival began. Now, in less than two years, over 100,000 souls had been won to Christ. God had given Evan what he had asked for. It had cost Evan everything, including his health.

In 1906, Evan was speaking at a Christian Conference when he shared some very strange ideas. He said he wanted to suffer like Jesus did. He wanted to experience everything that

Jesus had on the Cross; in short he wanted to be killed on a cross. Lots of the Christians there thought this was very strange. Soon afterwards Evan had his final breakdown.

While at the conference, Mrs. Jessie Penn-Lewis introduced herself to him. She would soon take Evan away from Wales for a long time.

Chapter 13
The Woman Who Controlled Him
★ ★ ★ ★

Mr. and Mrs. Penn-Lewis

Pulled from God's Call

Mrs. Penn-Lewis was a minister from England. She had been turned away from Wales because of her strange teachings. When she heard

Evan talk about suffering with Jesus she was delighted. She had thought the same thing.

She came alongside Evan and told him how he was being abused because of his teaching. Wherever he went she followed him. In less than a month Evan suffered his fourth and most serious nervous breakdown. When it happened Mrs. Penn-Lewis was there and ready to act.

She wrote to some of the ministers in Wales saying, "I will never return to your nation, because I have been so hurt by you. You have been so mean to me because of what Evan Roberts and I believe. I think it is best for Evan to stay away from Wales. After all he is too tired to do anything."

With that, she quickly took Evan to her home in England where she lived with her husband. They built a new home for themselves and made part of the home especially for Evan to stay in. He had his own private staircase in the house leading to a bedroom and a prayer room.

For the first time in his life, Evan was living outside of his home country of Wales. He had given his life for his nation and spent hours in prayer. He had turned down invitations to speak that came from all over the world and now he was not even living in his own country.

When Evan moved in to the Penn-Lewis estate, he was sent to his bed and stayed there for many months. Evan *was* tired and he did need to rest. This got him away from the work and allowed him to rest. But Mrs. Penn-Lewis was not just there to look after him. She wanted to use him to help her own ministry.

Was it All a Mistake?

Every day she went to see Evan. Every day she told him what he had done wrong in his meetings. "It was all emotional," she told him. "When you thought the Holy Spirit was speaking through you, you were being deceived."

Day after day she told him how he had

been deceived and needed to repent. The Holy Spirit had given Evan some of His gifts, as described in the Bible. The word of knowledge and gift of prophecy were working through his ministry, but Mrs. Penn-Lewis told him it was not from God.

Evan decided never to move in the supernatural again. If he stopped to think about it he would have thought of the thousands of people who had been saved by the gifts God had given him. But Mrs. Penn-Lewis did not allow him to think for himself.

When one minister came to interview Evan, she stopped him and had him thrown out of the house. Many letters that were sent to him were never answered. After a while people began to think that she was not even passing the letters on to him.

Bit by bit she was trying to control every part of his life.

Recovering ... Slowly

Eventually a friend was allowed to visit Evan. He was also a minister and he prayed for Evan. Slowly, over a long time, Evan's body started to recover. It took a whole year before he was even able to get out of his bed and walk. When he finally did walk his doctor told him never to preach again. He could counsel people, but not preach. "Your body will not be able to take the strain," he told Evan.

Mrs. Penn-Lewis was delighted. She fully agreed with the doctor, "You are not to preach," she ordered. Now she could really use Evan to help her ministry. Everyone wanted to hear from him and she could use his name to make her ministry bigger and better.

Evan was shielded from bad news to help him get better. So when Evan's mom became sick, nobody told him. Evan also cut himself off from his family. One time, when his dad traveled all the way to Leicester to speak with him, Evan refused to even see him! He never wrote to his family.

Evan wanted his whole life to be caught up in the spiritual world so much, that he forgot he was still living in this world. When people were with him they found it very hard to talk with him. Evan didn't want to be seen in public or to preach, he was happy just spending time praying.

Working for a Woman

Evan was still caught up by Mrs. Penn-Lewis. He thought she was a spiritual woman who understood God more than most people did. She persuaded him to translate her books into Welsh and to make her book into tracts for people to read in English.

Evan had been a mighty revivalist, now he was just doing paper work for a woman who was spiritually misguided. The same thing happened to many of the heroes in the Bible. Samson was led astray by a woman, Elijah suffered under

Jezebel. Evan was being pulled from his calling.

In 1908, Evan started a Prayer Watch. He invited people to join him to pray. For a few months they met together, until Evan decided he would rather pray by himself. Jesus warns us not to cut ourselves off from people, but in this difficult time in Evan's life this is just what he did. So many people had been looking to Evan and wanting something from him, he was now very happy to be in the background and out of sight.

Mrs. Penn-Lewis started a magazine that circulated around the world and Evan wrote in it each month. When she became sick in 1912, Evan wrote the whole magazine for her. When she was better she closed it down. In its place she started a conference for Christian Workers. She didn't let Evan speak there. But he did go to pray and to counsel people.

As he counseled people they were amazed. It seemed like Evan knew exactly what was going on inside them. He seemed to know what they needed to do to put things right. Evan still had little understanding about spiritual gifts, but in his counseling he was using the gift of discernment.

In later years, Evan started to teach small groups of people about prayer. Whenever he was teaching he started to come alive again. People saw a glimpse of the Evan Roberts who had helped many people to live for God.

Betraying the Revival

Around this time Evan was not sure what had happened in the revival. Mrs. Penn-Lewis had totally confused him. He wrote a book with Mrs. Penn-Lewis called "War on the Saints." The book told how believers could be deceived by Satan. The revival in Wales was written about in the book. It stated that Evan Roberts had been tricked by Satan.

When the book was finished the people in

Wales could not believe it! How could the man they looked upon so highly think that God was not in the revival. Many of them had been saved through the revival. Parts of the revival were certainly a bit strange, but God was there changing people and their lives. Surely nobody could disagree with that. Especially not one of the leaders of the revival!

Evan didn't really believe what had been written in the book. One year later he said, "The book, 'War on the Saints' is a failed weapon which has confused and divided the Lord's people."

Meanwhile, back in Wales, the Christians were confused and divided!

Chapter 14
Evan the Intercessor

★ ★ ★ ★

Evan Roberts

The Revival Burns Out

While Evan Roberts was all by himself, the revival in Wales had carried on without him. Over time it started to fizzle out. The revival had been hard work for the believers and many churches were quite happy to get back to their normal program. Some church leaders even started to speak against the revival. These leaders spoke about Evan and pointed out how he was not around. Some even spoke about the noise in the meetings and said it was wrong for a church meeting to be so noisy.

Whenever God moves there will always be people who say it is not God. There will also be people who try to stop it, just like the Pharisees did to Jesus. In fact, Jesus warns us that this will happen. The key thing to look at is the fruit of a work—what happens because of it.

The revival in Wales had good fruit. Thousands of people were choosing to follow Jesus. Whole communities were now happier and more peaceful. God had brought about deep and lasting change.

Churches Push New Believers Away

Meanwhile the new converts were not looked after very well. Most churches did not give them any special Bible teaching or support, they just let them get by on their own. When some people wanted to go out on mission, people thought they were strange.

They didn't realize this was what Jesus told us to do when He left the Earth. The strange believers were actually the ones who *didn't* want to go, not the ones who did.

In one church, some of the revivalists who went to every church meeting and supported the church, set up a school to teach the poor people in the area about Jesus. The church told them to stop the school or be kicked out of the church. The people prayed and knew God wanted them to carry on, so the church leaders kicked them out. The revivalists set up a Gospel Hall so that they could do what God had told them to do. Many halls of this kind were set up all over Wales.

The revivalists' passion for God continued, but gradually lots of the Gospel Halls got stuck in a routine. Evan Roberts had left them and they became tired of fighting the fight of faith with little or no encouragement from strong leadership.

Praying Again

What they didn't know was that Evan hadn't left them completely. He was spending his time praying. Before the revival had started, Evan Roberts had spent a lot of time in prayer. During the revival he spent time in prayer too. Often during a meeting he would cut himself off from everything that was going on around him and talk with God. As he spoke he would pray for someone in the meeting who was not saved, or who needed help from God. The Holy Spirit showed Evan what to pray for.

This prayer life was one of the big ministries that God had given Evan. So when Evan was by himself, shut away in Mrs. Penn-Lewis' house, he would spend a lot of time in prayer. He got excited when he taught people about prayer. He sometimes even enjoyed praying with people. But his greatest joy was to be alone with God in prayer.

"What I really want is for my life to be one long prayer from when I wake up in the morning until when I go to bed at night. I don't want to stop praying, even for a minute."

For eight years Evan didn't leave his home, but spent hour after hour in prayer.

Jesus is Coming Back

As Evan prayed more and more, one thing became more important in his mind. Jesus would be coming back soon. The more Evan prayed, the more he realized that the Church was supposed to be waiting for Jesus.

Although Jesus didn't come back while Evan was alive, he was right to live this way. When we expect Jesus to be back soon it changes the whole way we live. We live life differently. Jesus had said He would return and we should live as if His return could happen today.

Jesus will come back for a Church that is ready for Him, a Church that is united together and living fully for God. So Evan put all his energies into encouraging the Church to unite and to get ready for Jesus. By the end of 1913, Evan was writing to people and churches to encourage them that they would soon be meeting with Jesus. People all over the world read Evan's warnings.

Many people laughed at Evan. (Don't forget, they also laughed at Noah while he was building the ark.) Those who looked by faith would have known that Evan was right. Jesus told us to be ready and to expect Him back at any moment.

For many of the young people who were listening to Evan's words they were about to meet Jesus far sooner than they expected. Less than a year later, on July 28, 1914, the First World

War began. In England alone, nearly one million people were killed, with millions more dying all over the world. Many of the converts from the Welsh Revival had found salvation just in time, before they were killed in the war trenches.

When the war ended in 1918 Evan did less and less work for Mrs. Penn-Lewis.

God Heals Today

By 1925, he was living in Brighton, in the South of England. Evan bought himself a typewriter and started to write booklets. Many of his booklets were about missions. They were badly written so not many people bought them, but he did say some great things.

He was also learning more about God during all this time.

One day Evan heard that the daughter in the family he was staying with was sick. She had tonsillitis and needed an operation. As soon as Evan heard this he felt he had to pray for her. As Evan prayed the thought kept coming to him that the girl was going to die. Evan spoke to her father, knowing that he prayed a lot too.

"I keep thinking that your daughter is going to die. We must pray for her."

By that time tonsil removal was a routine operation. The father didn't really listen to Evan. But Evan kept on praying. A few days later she came home alive and well. The tonsils had been removed and the operation had been a complete success.

The girl went back to the hospital for a checkup a while later. As she walked into the hospital a nurse came up to her. She had a huge smile on her face and said to the girl, "It's so good to see you! We really thought you were going to die. When we were operating on you, your heart stopped three times and we had to pump it with our own hands. Had we known we would have given you a different medicine to put you to sleep!"

Evan had been right and God had used him to pray for her healing. Evan had discovered God's power of healing, through prayer. It would not be long before others would see God move through him in this way.

All through the years that Evan was in England, he never forgot his homeland in Wales. He still loved Wales more than any other place.

Chapter 15
Back to Wales

★ ★ ★ ★

An older Evan Roberts

We Need Revival

Wales had not forgotten about Evan Roberts either, even though they did not understand him or know what he was doing. David Lloyd George was a Welsh man through and through. He was also the Prime Minister of Great Britain. When he saw the problems in Wales he said, "We need another revival."

People started to talk about revival again. People had been distracted by the First World War, now they started to think about their souls and spirits again. When one of Evan's friends became a minister in Wales, Evan wrote him a letter to congratulate him. "Can I send this letter to the newspaper to be printed," the minister asked.

"You may," Evan responded.

So, for the first time in ten years the people of Wales heard something from the man who had led the revival. "He's still around, he's still following God," they said."Maybe he could lead a revival again."

The Voice of Revival Speaks Again

In 1926, Evan's dad became sick. Evan went home to be with his family. He had refused to speak to them during the ten years he was in England, but now they were just happy to have him back. They could have been hurt because he had rejected them, but they were just happy to see him again.

While he was there people asked him to speak in the local chapel. As Evan walked up into the pulpit everyone examined him carefully. The man who had left Wales ten years before had been young, this man now looked old. He had changed so much since they last saw him, but when he started to speak they recognized him immediately. The Holy Spirit still spoke through Evan. The people became excited as they remembered the revivals that had happened before. "Could we have another revival?" they wondered.

Word spread around Wales, people began to pray for God to move again. The Church started to wake up to its memories of the past revival. Evan's dad was not getting better. Evan went home more often to see him. Each time he went into Wales people wondered if this would be the day when a new revival would start, but it was not quite time yet.

Back at Home

When Mrs. Penn-Lewis died in 1927, Evan moved back to Wales for good. Evan was so happy to be back in his homeland and he was able to spend more time with his family. He moved into his own home, paid for by some local businessmen and started to build a new life in Wales.

He spent a lot of time with his father, looking after him and praying for him, until his dad died a year later.

Revival at the Funeral

Evan had loved his dad. In fact, Evan's dad had been loved by most people who knew him. So when the funeral began the little chapel was full of people. Everyone was wearing black and the atmosphere was very heavy. People were lost in their own thoughts and memories about Evan's dad. They knew they would never see him on Earth again. They were quiet and sad.

As the service continued they sang hymns to God and prayed together. Then one man stood up to share his memories. As he started to speak, people finally let their grief come out. Tears trickled down the face of many of the listeners. It was the saddest moment so far.

Suddenly Evan leapt out of his seat and interrupted the whole service. Everyone looked up and saw Evan standing at the front of the chapel.

He started to pray,

"Oh God, we are not here to mourn my dad's death. He is not dead. You have raised him back to life again. We should be celebrating what you have done. This is not a death this is a resurrection. Let's act like it!"

As he spoke, people felt something like electricity go through them. His words really encouraged them and they knew that he was right. This wasn't Evan speaking; it was the Holy Spirit speaking through him. Death was not the end of life, but the start of life in Heaven with God. It was like Heaven was opened up and God was near them all. It felt like a revival was about to start right there in the middle of the funeral service.

The funeral continued, but now there was a new note of joy that carried through to the end of the service as they celebrated the life on Earth of a believer and his resurrection in Heaven. Once again, Evan Roberts had been used by God to get people focusing on Him. One man thought that if Evan had continued on, revival would have broken out in the middle of the funeral service. The people of Wales would not have to wait much longer for God to answer their dreams and prayers for another revival.

Chapter 16
The Little Revival

★ ★ ★ ★

Moriah Chapel

A Call for Revival

During the Welsh Revival Evan had traveled around with a small band of singers. After the revival many of them had left the village to get married or to find work. Mary Davies had stayed, however, and she had given her life to looking after those who had given their lives to Jesus where the revival had broken out in Moriah Chapel.

She had never married, but quietly went on serving God. Her family ran the local post office and she was busy in the church, in prayer and with her artwork. Then in the fall of 1928, Mary felt God speaking to her. "Gather together some faithful believers and pray for revival."

Mary spoke to some of her friends and they met in the old post office to pray.

Four people met to pray at the first meeting in November. The next time they met, double the number of people came. Before long the numbers doubled again and again.

They soon had to move to a larger room and not just because they were growing in numbers, but there was a growing excitement within them that the Holy Spirit had called them all together because He wanted to do something special again. The Holy Spirit spoke to Mary again, "Write to Evan Roberts and ask him to come and hold some meetings here." Mary obeyed the Holy Spirit again.

When Evan opened the letter he, too, knew that the Holy Spirit wanted him to go. Immediately he sent a telegram back to Mary. When the telegram arrived in the post office, one of Mary's sisters was working there. She picked up the telegram, left the shop and went running down the street.

"He's coming. Evan Roberts is coming back," she shouted. The word spread across the village and by the time the first meeting began many people came to hear him.

Evan Roberts is Back

The first meeting took place in the old post office where Mary had been praying. "My friends," Evan said, "revival is not about me. It is a work of God's Holy Spirit. That's why God says, 'It's not by might, not by power but by my Spirit.' Don't look to me for a revival, but look to God."

Many people who had fallen away from God came back to Him again. It was a very exciting time. More meetings followed and they soon moved into Moriah Chapel. Evan quickly slipped back into the mode of the radical revivalist.

"Someone is blocking this meeting because of their disobedience. The meeting will not go on until they have owned up." Before long someone would own up to their disobedience and the meeting would continue with a new freedom.

One time when Evan was encouraging everyone to pray for their friends and relatives by name a man walked into the chapel. He heard his wife and daughter praying for him. The next thing he knew he was on his knees crying out to God for forgiveness.

One day a couple came to Evan. "Will you pray for our child?" Evan took the child into the old post office and started to pray for him. As he did so, light flooded into the room and everyone present felt the Holy Spirit there.

The family and friends started to pray and praise God. They were making so much noise that people ran into the room from the post office to join in. As the noise of praise grew louder, shoppers ran across the street to come and be a part of it. So many people gathered that they spilled onto the street and blocked the roads.

The intensity of the previous revival was back.

A New Anointing

But there was also something new. Now Evan was praying for the sick and casting out demons as well. One man was being convicted by God, but he was also bound by a demon. Evan commanded the devil to leave the man. As Evan prayed a loud scream came out of the man and he started to roll around on the floor. By the time Evan had finished praying the man sat up totally free. For the rest of his life he served God and reached out to the lost.

One minister was suffering from a serious illness that was gradually killing him. Evan laid hands on him and prayed for him to be healed. The minister was healed and went on preaching for twelve more years.

So the revival continued. Healings, conversions, deliverance and amazing answers to prayer got everybody talking. All the gifts of the Spirit were being shown, except for the gift of tongues. Evan refused to let people speak in tongues in the meetings. Of course, in the first revival he had used the gift of prophecy, and the gift of the word of knowledge, he used these gifts in this little revival too.

Some people thought he had become a Pentecostal. Really he had just become closer to Jesus from spending day after day in prayer.

Evan tried to explain to people why he was using the gifts now, but had avoided them before. "In the previous revival the gifts of the Spirit were in Scripture but the children of that revival were not ready for them. Some of them would have chased after the gifts instead of after God. But now they are ready."

Making Disciples out of the Converts

It wasn't just the gifts of the Spirit that marked this revival as different. This time Evan spent a lot of time teaching in Bible classes. In the first revival many of the people in Wales knew the Bible, they just didn't know God. But the lack of teaching meant that some of the believers had stopped following God. This time Evan set up a Bible class to teach the new believers.

After several weeks of meetings everyone knew that God had visited them in a very special way. Everyone wanted Evan to stay around longer, but Evan retired from public ministry.

"People will never understand me. For twenty-five years I have given my life to prayer. When preaching I can only reach a few people at a time, but when praying I can reach the whole world."

He was fifty years old and still had many years ahead of him, but not many of them would be lived in public.

Chapter 17
The Final Chapter
★ ★ ★ ★

A monument for Evan Roberts

A Life of Prayer

Evan continued to pray for the rest of his life. When he was on vacation, he would visit the places where revival had broken out before. In many places it hardly looked like a revival had taken place. But wherever he went, God encouraged him that a great work had taken place.

In one place an elderly lady came up to him to shake his hands. "Mr. Roberts, thank you so much. Because of you, my son gave his life to the Lord before he was killed in the First World War."

Evan didn't hide away like he used to. He loved to chat with people and he loved spending time with poets and writers. In fact, Evan started to write poems again. He wrote poems for friends, poems in letters, and poems just to write down what was in his heart.

Evan spent a lot of time praying for people as well. Sometimes he would pray for people and then write them a letter to let them know he had been praying for them.

"How did you know what our needs were?" people would often ask. Evan was simply obeying his lifelong friend and partner, the Holy Spirit.

Depression Comes and Goes

At times Evan felt depressed. He couldn't shake this feeling that something was wrong. The Church just wasn't living for God, but there was an even darker shadow to come. Then in 1939, the 2nd World War began. Every day, Evan would sit in his room reading the papers. Each paper for the next five years brought reports of death and destruction. Evan was now old and alone. His poetry at this time of his life was sad, and at times it seemed he even tired of praying.

"People are more worried about bombs than God's judgment. They don't even think about Heaven and hell. Heaven doesn't excite them and hell doesn't scare them. We are in a sad state," he wrote.

Each time he felt despair; he managed to find joy with God. One day he saw builders rebuilding the bombed out structures after the war, and he realized that God was going to rebuild His Church too. Life would come back to the Church again.

Evan enjoyed the last few years of his life, going to the theatre and watching sports. Some people wondered if he had fallen away from God, but Evan kept his focus on God's Kingdom.

In May, he spent every day in bed. In September, 1950, he could only write one word in his diary, "ill." This illness was the beginning of the end of his life on Earth. At the start of 1951, Evan Roberts died and was buried on January 29 behind Moriah Chapel.

When he died the Western Mail newspaper that had been the first to write about the revival many years ago, said: "He was a man who had experienced strange things. In his youth, he had seemed to hold the nation in the palms of his hands. He endured strains and underwent great changes of opinion and outlook, but his religious convictions remained firm to the end."

Lessons from Evan Roberts' Life

Evan lived his whole life for God. He did not spend much of his life in public, but whenever he spoke his words shook the people who heard him. Many people turned to God through his ministry, which must be set in the context of the run up to the two World Wars that devastated nations.

In prayer he had asked for 100,000 converts in Wales and God had given him that, but Evan had not looked after his own body. He had suffered from lack of sleep that led to illness and depression.

Evan had everything he needed from God to shake the world, but he didn't seem to have the emotional strength to be able to cope with it. He didn't let papers take his photo or interview him because he did not want to be seen, but his weaknesses meant that people ended up looking at him more.

We will never know what he prayed to God when he was on his own, or the effects of his prayers. But we do know that the Welsh revival in 1904 led to many other revivals around the world. Many people who visited the revival in Wales carried it back to their own countries. One man went to India where there was a great revival. Others went to America.

In 1906, God brought a great revival in Azusa Street. Some of the leaders of the Azusa Street revival wrote to Evan and Evan wrote back to let them know he was praying for them to see revival. From this revival the gifts of the Spirit spread across the Church worldwide.

Prayer is powerful. The more you pray, the closer you will get to God. As you read the Bible you will see God's heart and His power. Evan was just one man, but God used him powerfully in Wales and beyond.

God can use you too, to bring revival to a whole nation.

To do it successfully you need to be strong in your body and soul as well as your spirit. To be strong in spirit you need to seek God with all your heart in prayer. To be strong in your body you need to eat well, exercise, and rest. To be strong in your soul you need good, godly friends around you who you can share together with, and listen to their warnings.

Dream big dreams of how God can use you and have great faith that He is able to do more than you can ask or even imagine. Then ask God to prepare you now for your future destiny. Be an intercessor and a revival carrier!

Bible Study for Young Generals

Read Ephesians 6:10-13

1. This passage tells us we are all in a battle. Who are we fighting against?

2. What are we fighting for?

3. What do we have to do so that we will be able to keep standing?

4. What can we learn from Evan Roberts to help us to stand?

Bibliography

Brynmor Pierce Jones, *An instrument of Revival: The complete life of Evan Roberts 1878-1951* (South Plainfield, NJ: Bridge Publishing 1995)

Brynmor Pierce Jones, *Voices from the Welsh Revival 1904-1905* (Bridgend, Wales: Evangelical Press of Wales 1995)

Roberts Liardon, *God's Generals: Why they succeeded and why some failed* (Tulsa, OK: Whitaker House 1996)

David Matthews, I Saw the Welsh Revival (Chicago, IL: Moody Press 1951)

Daniel Mydrim Phillips, Evan Roberts: The Great Welsh Revivalist and His Work (London, UK: Marshall Brothers 1923)

Authors' Contact Information

Roberts Liardon

United States office:
P.O.Box 2989, Sarasota, FL 34230
E-mail: Info1@robertsliardon.org
www.robertsliardon.org

United Kingdom/European office:
Roberts Liardon Ministries
22 Notting Hill Gate, Suite 125
London W11 3JE, UK

Olly Goldenberg
BM Children Can, London WC1N 3XX, UK
info@childrencan.co.uk
www.childrencan.co.uk

The Spy Kit

The Spy Kit helps children aged 5-11 to pray by themselves at home. Inside you will find:

1. *The Spy Track CD* with quirky characters and bouncy songs, children learn a model of prayer. They then get to put it into practice as they pray along with the CD.

2. *The Spy Guide*. This booklet goes with the spy track. It is full of puzzles, prayer pointers and pages of space to make their own prayer notes.

3. *An invisible ink pen* to write invisible things, which may seem pointless until you realise there is a special light on the pen which makes invisible things visible.

4. *A zero gravity pen (sort of)*. With this you could write a note on the moon.

Children aged 5-11 will love this fun interactive resource that really does get them praying!

Title: The Spy Kit

EAN: 0799475676987

Available from www.childrencan.co.uk